Esperanza Rising
by Pam Muñoz Ryan

A Study Guide by Ray Moore

Contents

An Introduction.. 1

Dramatis Personæ 3

Settings.. 6

Genre.. 6

Narrative Voice.. 7

Themes 8

Symbols.. 12

Study Guide... 15

Vocabulary 30

Appendix 1: Reading Group Use of the Study Guide Questions....................... 38

Appendix 2: Literary Terms relevant to this text... 40

Notes on Graphic Organizers 43

Plot graph for *Esperanza Rising*... 44

Developing perspectives on the situation which initiates the action in
the novel... 45

Plot development 46

Esperanza Then and Now 48

How Miguel shows that he cares for Esperanza............................ 49

To the Reader 51

Esperanza Rising by Pam Muñoz Ryan

An Introduction

Plot Summary

Esperanza Rising (2000) tells the story of Esperanza Ortega between her thirteenth and fourteenth birthdays. Raised in Mexico to a life of privilege on her family's extensive ranch, her life is shattered when her father is murdered. Because of her father's evil brothers, Esperanza's mother, Señora Ortega, is robbed of her inheritance, and Esperanza and Mama are forced to move to the United States in search safety of and a way to earn a living. It is hard for young Esperanza to adapt to a life in which she no longer has wealth and servants, particularly since she and her mother can only find employment as field-laborers in the San Joaquin Valley, California. The novel traces a difficult year (1930-1) in Esperanza's life, one that sees her adapt and mature, so that, by the end of the novel, we feel that she has become a better person.

Why Read this Book?

This novel has won multiple awards. Amazon.com gives it a 4.5 (out of 5) star rating based on over 800 reviews. Evidence suggests that the appeal of the novel goes well beyond students of Mexican heritage. Young readers who have recently immigrated into the US (particularly those who have fled violence) also empathize with Esperanza.

Important: Issues with this Book:

There is no bad language, no violence and no sex. The novel does challenge some current misconceptions about Mexicans living and working in California, and it shows the police and the immigration authorities acting illegally to break up a strike. This might shock some readers.

Graphic organizers:

Five graphic organizers are provided to enable the students to make notes. Some guidance is given which can be adapted depending on how the teacher wants them to be used.

Acknowledgements:

As always, I am indebted to the work of reviewers and critics. Where I am conscious of having taken an idea or a phrase from a particular author, I cite the source in the text: failure to do so is an omission which I will immediately correct if it is drawn to my attention. I believe that all quotations used in the book fall under the definition of 'fair use'. Once again, if I am in error on any quotation, I will immediately remove it if it is drawn to my attention.

A Study Guide

Preface:

A Study Guide is an *aid* to the close reading of a text; it is *never a substitute* for reading a text. This text deserves to be read reflectively. I have heard of a third grader (who had the novel read to her by her mother) who talked enthusiastically about this novel, and I have myself experienced an adult reading circle discussing the book in great detail. Knowing quite where to 'pitch' a study guide is not easy, but I suggest that, like the author, we expect a lot of our students.

Neither the study questions nor the graphic organizers have answers provided. This is a deliberate choice. Even 'suggested' answers would limit the exploration of the text by readers themselves which is the primary aim. I found in my classroom that students frequently came up with answers I had not even considered, and, not infrequently, that they expressed their ideas better than I could have done. The point of this Guide is to open up exploration of the text not to close it down by providing 'already made answers.' Teachers *do not need* their own set of answers in order to evaluate their students' responses.

Page numbers (indicated in parenthesis) refer to the Scholastic edition of 2000.

Esperanza Rising by Pam Muñoz Ryan

Dramatis Personæ

The Ortega Family:

The Ortegas are wealthy landowners in Aguascalientes, a state in north-central Mexico. Their farm is called El Rancho de las Rosas.

Papa (Sixto)

Esperanza's father has a deep love for the land and teaches Esperanza to feel that it is a living thing. Although he is wealthy, he is an enlightened man who treats his workers well. Shortly before Esperanza's thirteenth birthday, he is murdered by bandits while working on the ranch.

Mama (Ramona)

Esperanza's mother is devastated by the murder of her husband and by the resulting loss of her home. However, she takes control of her own future by refusing to marry her corrupt brother-in-law, Tío Luis, because that would separate her from Esperanza. Ramona is a great source of support to Esperanza, helping her to adjust to the changed life that she has after her father's death, until she becomes seriously ill with Valley Fever and has to be hospitalized.

Esperanza (Anza)

Esperanza is six years old at the start of the novel. The daughter of a wealthy and loving family, her life is just about perfect, and she assumes that it will continue to be so. The death of her father just before her thirteenth birthday changes everything. Esperanza and her mother must move to America and begin their life again as migrant workers in California. It is important to remember that Esperanza, though very well educated at a private school, does not speak or read English. She is the protagonist of the novel because she must learn how to adjust to being a migrant worker in California; through struggling to survive she develops into a stronger, more caring and more mature person.

Abuelita

Esperanza's maternal grandmother teaches Esperanza the importance of perseverance. Due to an ankle injury, she has to stay behind in Mexico when Esperanza and Mama escape to California. Eventually, Miguel (see below) is able to bring her to the U.S.A. to rejoin her daughter and granddaughter.

Tío Marco

Papa's older brother is the Mayor of Aguascalientes. He is totally under the influence of his younger brother.

Tío Luis

Papa's other brother is president of the Bank in Aguascalientes. He is the main antagonist in the first few chapters of the novel. After Sixto's death, Tío Luis tries to force Ramona to marry him because he thinks that her popularity will help him in the political career he has planned. When she refuses, his men burn down her house, and he vaguely threatens more such regrettable 'accidents'. To escape him, Mama and Esperanza flee to America.

Characters who Esperanza knows in Mexico:
Alfonso
He is employed as the leader of the field-workers at El Rancho, but he is also Papa's close friend. When Sixto is killed, he makes arrangements for his family to travel to California to join his brother Juan, and by telling the camp owners that Ramona and Esperanza are members of his family, he makes it possible for them all to leave Mexico together.

Hortensia
Alfonso's wife, a Zapotec Indian from Oaxaca, is the housekeeper at El Rancho. She has always taken care of Esperanza (for example by bathing her). In California, their relationship, though always a loving one, changes considerably.

Miguel
Alfonso and Hortensia's son was Esperanza's childhood companion, and before she realized the vast difference in their wealth and social background Esperanza dreamed of marrying him. When she told him that this could never be because of the river of class that divided them, he was hurt and bitter. Miguel develops many of Papa's qualities - he is patient, determined, and kind. He loves trains and dreams of becoming a mechanic on the railroad. He believes that in the United States he will have the chance to be something more than a servant.

Marisol Rodríguez
She is Esperanza's best friend in Mexico, but they lose contact when Esperanza and her mother have to move to California.

Characters who Esperanza knows in California:
Juan
Alfonso's brother welcomes everyone into his home in California where he lives with his family in a small cabin in a workers' camp owned by the farm company. He also lies to the owners telling them that Esperanza and Mama are his cousins. This is the only way they could have got into the camp.

Josefina
She becomes an important role model for Esperanza particularly after Mama falls ill. Despite her poverty, she is a good mother and raises her children to be happy despite their poverty.

Isabel
Juan and Josefina's daughter is only "about eight years old" (86), but she is much more mature that Esperanza because of her years of experience living in the camps. She is in awe of what she has heard of Esperanza's privileged life in Mexico, but unlike Marta (see below) she does not resent it. Actually, she loves

to listen to Esperanza telling stories about her privileged past. Her dreams are to go to school so that she can learn English and learn to read.

Pepe and **Lupe**

Isabel's twin baby brother and sister need someone to care for them and when Isabel starts school this becomes one of Esperanza's first duties in the farm camp. It is very challenging at first since Esperanza has always been the one being looked after, but see soon masters it.

Marta

A teenage girl who is the same age as Miguel, she lives in an adjacent camp with her widowed mother, Ava. One of the first things she tells Esperanza is that her father was killed in the Mexican Revolution fighting against the rich land-owners like Esperanza's father. At first, Marta has the role of antagonist: she publicly mocks Esperanza for her privileged upbringing and her lack of experience doing manual labor. Marta fights for the rights of migrant workers and is one of the organizers of a strike. When immigration officials break up the strike, however, Esperanza helps Marta to hide from the police.

The photo was on the *Mexican Migration* Wiki. There were no details of its author. I assume that, given the age of the image, it must now be in the public domain and not subject to copyright. If I am in error, I will immediately remove it.

Spoiler alert!

If you are reading the novel for the first time, you *may* wish to go straight to the Study Questions and come back to these sections later.

Settings

The first four chapters are set in the state of Aguascalientes, Mexico. It is a beautiful agricultural region. However, there is lingering resentment in the country against the rich landowners, and bandits are an ever-present threat.

The remainder of the story is set in the San Joaquin Valley in California. This is an even more beautiful place, but the land is owned by very rich individuals and co-operations who exploit the manual workers who live in very basic camps. The action takes place in the early 1930s, the decade of the Great Depression and the Dust Bowl. In a complete reversal of fortune, in California, Esperanza, whose father was a big landowner, finds herself to be poor and has to work for the rich landowners.

Genre

Genre is defined as the class (or category) into which a work of art can be placed by its content, forms, technique, etc. In describing a novel as a Western, or a Spy Thriller, of a Detective Mystery, we are describing its genre.

Bildungsroman (The Coming of Age Novel)

A *Bildungsroman* tells the story (often, but not always, in the first person) of the growing up of a young, intelligent, and sensitive person who goes in search of answers to life's questions (including the biggest question of all: who they actually *are*) by gaining experience of the adult world from which they have before been protected by their youth. The novel tells the story of the protagonist's experiences in the world and of the inner, psychological process of his/her growth and development as a human being.

Examples of this genre: *Great Expectations* and *David Copperfield* by Charles Dickens, *Sons and Lovers* by D. H. Lawrence, *A Portrait of the Artist as a Young Man* by James Joyce, *The Catcher in the Rye* by J. D. Salinger, etc., etc.

Historical Fiction

The author tells us that this novel is a fictionalized version of her own grandmother's story and that she added to her family history by research from primary sources in order to get the historical details right. The book begins in 1924 in Aguascalientes, Mexico, a relatively prosperous time prior to the Great Depression, the start of which is dated to the Stock Market Crash of October, 1929.

It is late in the year 1930 when Esperanza and her mother become immigrations to California, where they move into a camp for farm workers.

Esperanza Rising by Pam Muñoz Ryan

While they are there, they begin to see the first movement into California of Okies – poor people from the Oklahoma and Texas panhandles and from neighboring sections of Kansas, Colorado, and New Mexico whose lands were suffering a drought that would lead, in 1934, to the Dust Bowl.

Magical Realism

In the Q & A at the back of the book, Muñoz says that some of her writing falls into the genre 'magical realism' which Merriam Webster defines as "a literary genre or style associated especially with Latin America that incorporates fantastic or mythical elements into otherwise realistic fiction." *Esperanza Rising* begins with two characters lying on the ground establishing a mystical union with the earth which is clearly described as a living being. Twice Esperanza flies. Of course, it could be argued that Muñoz describes only Esperanza's intense *feeling* that she is floating in the air. The description is, however, very realistic and matter of fact.

Narrative Voice

Esperanza Rising is written in the third person by an anonymous narrator who presents virtually everything from the perspective of the protagonist. The narrator knows that Esperanza is a very limited and selfish girl at the start of the story but also that she is fundamentally good and that people can change. The tone is deliberately inspirational. (Note: By calling Esperanza 'limited' I mean that she has only experienced the privileged life of the wealthy and that, as a result, there are certain emotions that she has never felt and does not really understand. To put it simply, Esperanza is not a fully developed human being. She is limited by her deep sense of entitlement.)

Themes

Family

Esperanza's relationship with her father, mother, and grandmother is central to who she is as a person. As a child, she is surrounded by wise people who love her and give her important lessons about personal responsibility, patience, bravery, understanding and kindness. Although she loses Papa and is forced to leave Abuelita in Mexico, Esperanza never forgets what they have taught her, and from her continuing relationship with her mother she learns to accept people as they are and to take a positive decision to be happy however hard her life becomes.

Living on El Rancho, Esperanza's life-experience has been very limited. When she moves to California it is as a member of Alfonso and Hortensia's family. She sees how they each look out for and depend upon each other, and she learns to take her place in this very different, but equally loving, family.

Esperanza learns the meaning of the Mexican proverb, "The rich person is richer when he becomes poor, than the poor person when he becomes rich." Her true wealth was never her parents' money and land, it was in the love that the members of her family had for each other and for her.

Perseverance and Starting Over

Speaking of having made a mistake in crochet stitching, Abuelita tells Esperanza, "Do not be afraid to start over" (15). Esperanza's grandmother uses the zigzag pattern in the blanket she is making (and which she asks Esperanza to complete for her) as a way of symbolizing the ups and downs of life: bad things happen to good people, but, as the Mexican proverb says, "He who falls today may rise tomorrow." At the time Abuelita tries to teach her, Esperanza lacks the patience to enjoy crocheting, let along the maturity to realize that she can start her life over following the disaster of her father's murder. However, she learns the hard way that, when life drops you into a valley, it is possible to pick yourself up and begin the climb back up. At the end of the story, we find Esperanza taking on the grandmother role by passing on Abuelita's advice to the younger Isabel.

There are many examples of Esperanza learning from her mistakes, especially about the way she should treat and feel about people who are poorer than herself. In California, Esperanza starts over financially (by getting out and doing manual labor) and socially (by taking on the responsibility of caring for her mother and earning the money needed for her grandmother to come from Mexico).

In the way it is structured, this novel is a reverse fairy tale: it is a riches to rags tale. Esperanza begins as a princess (a queen even) whom everyone adores, loses all of her wealth and social status, and ends up, poor but happy again, as a struggling immigrant worker laboring in the fields of the San Joaquin Valley. There is every indication that she will marry Miguel, whom she loves, and perhaps eventually earn enough money to buy a little white house and to enter the mainstream of American society (as the author's own grandmother did).

Hope

Both Esperanza and Miguel come to California with unrealistic hopes: Esperanza has convinced herself that her poverty is only temporary because her grandmother will soon recover her health, gain access to her savings from the bank, and come to California to 'rescue' Esperanza and Mama; Miguel believes that he will be judged solely on the basis of his skills and that he will be able to get a well-paid job. Isabel has the impossible hope that she will be named Queen of the May by her teacher. Each will be bitterly disappointed, but, as they adjust their expectations to the new reality, none of them gives up. Esperanza, whose name means 'hope' in Spanish, never gives up. She learns that, by being a hard and reliable worker, she can earn enough to save money, and Miguel shows no signs of giving up on being an engineer: despite setbacks, people can succeed. Isabel learns to speak and read English.

Patience

Papa used to tell Esperanza, "*Aguántate tantito y la fruta caerá en tu mano,*" "Wait a little while, and the fruit will fall into your hand" (2). He was telling her that she had to make an effort, but not to assume that success would be achieved overnight. He means that "To every thing there is a season, and a time to every purpose under the heaven: A time to be born, and a time to die; a time to plant, and a time to pluck up that which is planted; A time to kill, and a time to heal; a time to break down, and a time to build up; A time to weep, and a time to laugh; a time to mourn, and a time to dance..." (see *Ecclesiastes* 3:1-8). Basically, Papa believes that the earth is benevolent (i.e. it wants man to be happy): man lives as part of nature and must conform to the rhythm of the seasons. Patience is necessary.

Social Class in Mexico and the United States

In Mexico in the 1920s, social class was a rigid hierarchy of wealth, family heritage, and ethnicity (as reflected in skin tone). The poor feel that the Mexican Revolution has failed to address these fundamental (basic) inequalities. As she grows towards her teens, Esperanza comes to understand that a clear distinction exists between her and Miguel which means that, in Mexico, they can never marry: they stand on opposite sides of a river which they can never cross.

Of course, Esperanza and Miguel feel very differently about this. Miguel resents what is effectively a caste system and has no faith that change is possible. Rather naively, he sees the U.S.A. as a land of opportunity where individuals can rise by their own hard work and abilities. Miguel's description of the United States at the beginning of the novel illustrates the desire to rise socially that many Mexican immigrants associate with the American Dream. The reality proves to be somewhat different: he encounters racial discrimination combined with the exploitation of the poor by the rich. In California, even Mexicans who are well-educated and have skills (as Miguel does with engines) are grouped into a generalized Mexican stereotype. Thus, social mobility is almost impossible – almost, but not quite. The American Dream often seems beyond his reach, but he perseveres.

Esperanza is understandably quite content with her life of privilege: if she temporarily feels
sad when she realizes that she will never marry Miguel, she is soon excited by thinking about the fine, aristocratic men who will court her. In California, Esperanza finds herself among the really poor, and she struggles to adapt to the lower social class. Nevertheless, she eventually comes to accept her new position as she matures. It is easier for her to see the unfairness with which the workers in California are treated and to feel the injustice of it than it was for her to see these things at home in Mexico.

Racial Prejudice

Social division in Mexico depends on racial and ethnic bias: the wealthy are light-skinned; that is, they are descendants of the Spanish colonialists rather than of the indigenous Indians. Of course, Esperanza is ignorant about the pervasive (wide spread) racial prejudice in her country until it is explained to her by Miguel, and even then she dismisses it as "'just something that old wives say'" (80). Similarly, when she first starts living in the Mexican workers' camp in California, she does not experience racial prejudice because she lives only amongst poor Mexicans. However, when she and Miguel travel a long distance to Mr. Yakota's store, Miguel explains that it is because he is the only merchant who treats Mexican customers with respect. (Ironically, since he is a Japanese-American, Mr. Yakota will face internment during World War II).

Esperanza's understanding grows when the owners build an Oklahoma workers' camp with a swimming pool. Isabel is excited that those in the Mexican camp will be allowed to swim in the pool, but Esperanza is angry because they will only get to use the pool on Fridays, the day before the weekly cleaning, because of the common belief that Mexicans are dirtier than other races. In America, as in Mexico, racial and ethnic bias is dictated by skin-tone.

Exploitation of the Workers

To state the obvious, the farm owners want to get their crops harvested, processed and packed at the lowest possible cost, and, with more and more penniless workers moving west, they are in a strong position to drive down wages. That said, the novel gives a very balanced picture of the situation. The camp to which Esperanza goes is much better than most, and the company that runs it seems to treat the workers reasonably. On the other hand, the work camps are racially segregated, and the facilities in each camp are not the same (the new Okie camp, will, for example, have a swimming pool).

Esperanza is fortunate to work for a company which owns a lot of land and raises diverse crops so that workers are needed all year round. Marta and her mother have to follow the harvest moving from camp to camp, and such workers are more vulnerable to exploitation. Marta takes an active role in workers' strikes that aim to force the land owners to pay better wages and provide better living conditions. When this happens, the owners have no hesitation in employing the police to clear out the troublemakers and to deport them to Mexico – even if they are actually US citizens who have never been to Mexico in their lives. The description of a policeman ripping up a striker's citizenship papers is quite shocking – it offends Esperanza's sense of what is right and wrong.

Symbols

The trunk at the foot of Esperanza's bed

In this trunk, Esperanza stores linens "for *algun dia*, for someday" (10). Thus, trunk is used to symbolize the future that Esperanza envisages (dreams of) for herself: always living at home but married to a son of one of the riches families in Mexico. The trunk is totally destroyed by the fire at the ranch, symbolizing that this future is no longer possible – it just takes Esperanza a long while to accept that truth.

Abuelita's blanket

Abuelita's blanket is the only material object (artifact) that is present at the beginning of the novel (when Abuelita teaches Esperanza to crochet its zigzag pattern) and at the end (when, Abuelita's blanket having been finished by Esperanza, grandma teaches Isabel its mountains and valleys stitch). Near the start of the novel, Abuelita tells Esperanza, "Do not be afraid to start over" (15), which is exactly the advice that Esperanza passes onto Isabel on the novel's last line (253).

The mountains and valleys represent the obstacles and triumphs that are an inevitable part of life. Abuelita makes the symbolic meaning of the pattern plain when, forced by injury to go to the nuns while Mama and Esperanza escape, she tells her granddaughter, "Right now you are in the bottom of the valley and your problems loom big around you. But soon, you will be at the top of a mountain again. After you have lived many mountains and valleys, we will be together" (51). This proves to be both a realistic image for the challenges that Esperanza faces in her new life and a very optimistic prediction that she will overcome them and that all will finally be well.

By the time Abuelita rejoins Esperanza in California, the huge and colorful blanket is almost finished; Esperanza puts the final stitches in while her grandmother watches. She has used yarn given to her by her neighbors at the camp and included strands of her own and Abuelita's hair symbolizing how various people have helped her on her journey to become the person she now is.

The Phoenix

The phoenix is a bird from Egyptian and Greek mythology. Merriam-Webster defines a phoenix as "a legendary bird which according to one account lived 500 years, burned itself to ashes on a pyre [fire], and rose alive from the ashes to live another period; also: a person or thing likened to the *phoenix*." The phoenix is thus a symbol of rebirth. After Esperanza's family home burns down, Abuelita tells her, "Esperanza, do you remember the story of the phoenix, the lovely young bird that is reborn from its own ashes? ... We are like the phoenix ... Rising again, with a new life ahead of us" (49-50) Like the phoenix, Esperanza and her family are literally emerging from a fire that ought logically to have destroyed them, but it hasn't: it has purified them and made them stronger – at least this is what Abuelita wants Esperanza to believe – and it proves to be true.

When Esperanza has her second experience of 'flying', we read, "She let herself be lifted into the sky ... on the wings of the phoenix ... with the anticipation of dreams she never knew she could have ..." (249-50). Esperanza emerges from her ordeal by fire ready to begin her life over.

The River

When Esperanza wants a way of explaining the social divide that separates her from Miguel, she naturally thinks of a river. The narrator explains how she instinctively picks this symbol:

> But now that she was a young woman, she understood that Miguel was the housekeeper's son and she was the ranch owner's daughter and between them ran a deep river. Esperanza stood on one side and Miguel stood on the other and the river could never be crossed. (18)

Although Miguel is devastated when Esperanza explains this to him, he later tells her, "'You were right, Esperanza. In Mexico we stand on different sides of the river'" (37).

Miguel believes that in the U.S.A. everyone has an opportunity to get ahead no matter what their race, religion or social standing. This proves not to be true, but what does happen is that Esperanza becomes just as poor as Miguel. Not only that, but she begins to realize that Miguel's qualities make him someone to be admired not to be looked down upon. Near the end of her second 'flight', after they have both felt the heartbeat of the earth, "she flew over a river, a thrusting torrent that cut through the mountains" (250) and has a vision of herself and Miguel as children, eating mangos "on the same side of the river" (251). She reaches out for Miguel's hand, and "his touch held her heart to the earth" (251). Just as she overcame the mountains in her path, so Esperanza has overcome the river (both real and psychological) that threatened to separate her from the person she loves.

Gifts

Every year for her birthday, Papa gives Esperanza a beautiful doll. The one that he planned to give her on her thirteenth birthday is dressed in "a fine white batiste dress and a white lace mantilla over her black hair" and looks like an angel (28). When she first sees it, Esperanza hugs the doll to her chest. For her, it represents everything about her old vanished life: her father's love, his wealth, and above all the difference between the Ortegas and peasants. When a peasant girl on the train out of Mexico wants to touch it, Esperanza jerks it away because the girl is poor and dirty. Mama is ashamed and makes the girl a yarn doll.

Later Esperanza gives her beautiful doll to Isabel to make up for her friend's disappointment at not being Queen of the May. She knows that this is what her father would have wanted her to do, just as earlier she gives the little piñata which she has bought for Mama to the poor children of strikers. Esperanza has learned that it is the giving, not the receiving, of gifts that makes her happy.

Roses

Roses are a traditional symbol of love (as in the lines "O my Luve is like a red, red rose. / That's newly sprung in June" by Robert Burns). Of course, roses have thorns, and just before her father's murder Esperanza pricks her finger badly, representing the pain that she will have to go through before she achieves happiness. The fact that Miguel brings to California the roses that Papa planted for him and for Esperanza and that they thrive and grow in the new soil, symbolizes the fact that the love between the two will grow once each has freed him/herself from the restrictions of Mexican society.

Fruits and vegetables

Ryan says in the Q & A at the end of the book that she named the chapters after the fruits and vegetables that were important at the time the action occurred to reflect "that Esperanza's life was taking on the rhythm of the harvest," and that she revised the chapters to make their "headings more symbolic." Some of the symbolism is clear: onions represent Esperanza's bitter dislike of the camp, avocados represent her understanding that she is poor and that her life will never be what it once was, and preparing potatoes for planting represents the new life that Esperanza is making. (Rather than list what all of the symbols mean to me, I leave the reader to decide.)

Study Guide

This novel deserves to be read *reflectively*. The questions are not designed to test you but to help you to locate and to understand characters, plot, settings, issues, and themes in the text. They do not normally have simple answers, nor is there always one answer. Consider a range of possible interpretations - preferably by discussing the questions with others. Disagreement is to be encouraged!

Definitions of useful literary terms are given at the end of this chapter.

Aguascalientes, Mexico: 1924

This short chapter, or prologue, establishes the close relationship that Papa has with the land. It is not just that he *owns* a large ranch (though, of course, he does) but that he loves the land on which his family has farmed for generations. To him, the land is a living thing, and he wants Esperanza also to feel this mystical (religious) connection.

Las Uvas (Grapes): Six years later

Esperanza lives a life of wealth and privilege surrounded by people who really love her. Though she is presented sympathetically by the narrator, there are signs that she is somewhat spoilt. For example, she takes great delight in ceremonially cutting the first grapes of the harvest, but it is the field-workers who will do the hard work for three weeks. Esperanza's thoughts quickly move on to her approaching birthday and to the fiesta and the expensive presents which will mark it. Esperanza emerges as kind and loving but very limited (lacking the full range of human experience and emotion). She is naïve, innocent, over-protected, proud of her family's social position and has a feeling of entitlement.

The Mexican Revolution began in 1910. A number of groups, led by revolutionaries including Francisco Madero, Pascual Orozco, Pancho Villa and Emiliano Zapata, battled the government, and each other, for leadership of the nation and many people acted as lawless vigilantes, burning down ranches and killing those with money. Though a constitution was drafted in 1917 that ended dictatorship, established a constitutional republic, and formalized many of the reforms sought by these rebel groups, periodic violence continued into the 1930s. (Adapted from History.com)

1. How does the description of the *campesinos* contrast with the description of Esperanza? ("The August ... long black hair." 4-5) What point is the narrator making by the contrast?

2. When Esperanza thinks of marrying, she hopes that "her someday-husband would live with Mama and Para forever. Because she couldn't imagine living anywhere other than El Rancho de las Rosas. Or with any fewer servants. Or without being surrounded by the people who adored her" (8). What does this dream tell you about the character of Esperanza?

3. Esperanza remembers a time when she declared to her parents that she would marry Miguel.

- How did her parents react?
- Why did Esperanza change her mind about marrying Miguel?
- Comment on the way that she told Miguel of her changed view of their future.

4. What pieces of evidence make it clear to the reader that Papa is dead long before his body is brought back?

Esperanza Rising by Pam Muñoz Ryan

Las Papayas (Papayas)

The chapter opens with Esperanza dreaming that her father is still alive. Understandably, she is in denial, but she is soon hit by the shock of reality. Señor Rodríguez, Marisol's father, knocks on the door. He has come to deliver the papayas that Papa ordered for her birthday fiesta, and he has not heard about Papa's murder. Having to explain what happened to Papa actually helps Esperanza to accept the tragedy.

Tío Luis proposes marriage to Mama because he knows that the respect in which she is held by the people as the widow of Sixto Ortega will win him votes in his run for state governor. His ruthlessness comes out when she rejects him. He vaguely threatens to "'make things very difficult for you. Very difficult'" (32). While he claims to be treating Mama generously, he is actually blackmailing her.

5. There is something false about the way in which Esperanza behaves in public in the days following Papa's death. What is it? How is the conduct of the three Ortega women different when they are in private?
6. How do Tío Luis and Tío Marco gradually take Papa's place in the house? What are the visible signs that Esperanza notices?
7. The terms of Papa's will place his widow in a very difficult situation: she is left ownership of the house and of the profits of the annual grape harvest, but not the ownership of the land itself which passes to Tío Luis. Looking back on it now, it is obvious that Papa made a very bad choice in doing this. However, he acted from reasons dictated by his culture. Explain why he wrote the will that he did.
8. What reasons does Miguel give to Esperanza to explain his family's decision to move to the United States as soon as they are no longer needed by her mother? (In response, Esperanza declares to herself "'I won't ever leave here'" [38]. This certainty reflects both her relative immaturity and her naïve confidence that the family will always have money. In contrast, Miguel is more realistic.)
9. Papa planted two rose bushes side-by-side in the garden when Miguel and Esperanza were young children. The closeness of the plants represented how inseparable the two children were. How does the description of the two roses on page 35 symbolize the way in which their growing awareness of social class has created a gap between them? (Both plants, however, grow in the same ground, which indicates that perhaps something more important than money and social position unites them.)

Los Higos (Figs)

Mama buys time by pretending that she will not consider Tío Luis' proposal of marriage – though she really has no idea of accepting him. Mama shows that she is quickly adapting to the new reality. When she withdraws to talk about her options, she insists that Esperanza and Miguel should be there because they "'are old enough to hear the discussion'" (46).

Although Esperanza hates the idea of Tío Luis becoming her stepfather, she also hates the idea of giving up the life she has known. In this time of confusion, Abuelita is a great source of strength to Esperanza. Her grandmother tells Esperanza for the first time of the struggles she had when she came from Spain to Mexico at the same age, "'There were many hard times. But life was also exciting'" (49).

10. Esperanza hears the plan for herself and Mama to accompany Miguel's family to California, but she still does not fully understand how different her life will be there from what she has been used to. In picturing life in California, Esperanza imagines three details that are entirely unrealistic. (See page 50.) What are they?

11. Explain Esperanza's unintentionally comic misunderstanding of the significance of the clothes from the poor box at the convent.

12. What two symbols of hope does Abuelita offer to Esperanza in this chapter?

13. What might the figs at the end of the chapter symbolize?

Esperanza Rising by Pam Muñoz Ryan

Las Guayabas (Guavas)

Because the family has to get away secretly at night, even Esperanza's best friend, Marisol, could not be told that they were going and so Esperanza had no opportunity to say goodbye to her. Everything seems to be taken from her.

Cramped in the secret compartment in the bottom of the wagon, Esperanza begins to panic, but Hortensia takes her mind off the present by reminding her how brave she was on another occasion when Hortensia, Miguel, and Esperanza hid from bandits under her bed. This in turn leads to pleasant memories of the first-class train journey she took with Miguel – Papa's reward to him for saving Esperanza's life.

The actual journey on the train is an uncomfortable reality-check for Esperanza. Mama does her best to educate her daughter about the changes that will be necessary in their attitudes and their conduct to other people – not particularly successfully.

Miguel explains to Esperanza the ethnic basis of Mexico's class system: those who are wealthy are descended from the Spanish conquerors and often have lighter skin than the poor who are descended from the Native American population. Esperanza realizes that Miguel is right and feels guilty that she has never noticed this distinction before. Both Miguel and Esperanza share the idealistic belief that the U.S.A. is a country where anyone willing to work hard can make money irrespective of their ethnicity.

14. Talking of Papa's promise to get him a job on the Mexican railway, Miguel tells Esperanza, "'And he would have kept his promise. He … he always kept his promises to me'" (74). Explain the reason for Miguel's pause and hesitation.

15 Immediately after this, Esperanza notices that Miguel's eyes "were damp," and we are told, "She had never thought about how much her papa must have meant to Miguel" (74). Is Esperanza correctly interpreting Miguel's sadness? Explain.

16. What do you consider the most shameful and inexcusable of Esperanza's actions in this chapter?

17. What do you consider the most generous and kind of Mama's actions in this chapter?

18. Esperanza notices that, every time the train stops, Alfonso and Miguel carry something in an oilcloth out to a water trough to "dampen the bundle inside" (73). What do you imagine they are carrying?

Los Melones (Cantaloupes)

Once through Immigration, the families go to Los Angeles and from there they go on by truck. When they stop for lunch, Esperanza takes a walk on her own. She thinks about how Papa taught her to feel connected with the land, so she lies down to hear its heartbeat but is frustrated to hear nothing. In tears, she rolls onto her back on the ground and then suddenly feels as if she is drifting above it. Esperanza feels "untethered and frightened" (92).

Esperanza realizes that her past wealth and high social standing actually make some people dislike her before they even know her. Marta, a girl they pick up, is about Miguel's age. Marta's father died in the Mexican Revolution fighting for the rights of the poor, so she resents Esperanza. Marta is both more mature and more experienced than Esperanza. She is also politically partisan, being firmly on the side of the workers against the exploitation by the owners of which she has first-hand experience. Esperanza finds Marta's ideas and the strength of feeling behind them very challenging. There may, however, be another element to their rivalry. Marta is about Miguel's age, and Esperanza certainly sees her as a rival for Miguel's attention: "[an] unfamiliar feeling was creeping up inside Esperanza" (99). It is jealousy.

19. What does Esperanza notice about the way in which people are dealt with as they line up to go through Immigration?
20. Why is Esperanza so shocked about Isabel's description of where her family lived last year?
21. Reflecting on Isabel's happiness at the prospect of learning in English, Esperanza thinks it is a little thing. What is she not understanding?
22. What do you make of the incident where Esperanza feels herself to be flying above the earth with no connection to it? What might this symbolize?
23. What explanation does Martha give for the owners' policy of racially segregating the camps? Can you suggest any further explanation(s)?

Esperanza Rising by Pam Muñoz Ryan

Las Cebollas (Onions)

The first night and the following day at the camp is a shock for Esperanza. She cannot believe that she and Mama will be sharing a tiny two-room cabin with Hortensia, Alfonso, and Isabel. To Esperanza, the cabin seems inferior to the servants' quarters at El Rancho and more like the horse stables on the ranch.

Left with Isabella to mind the babies, Pepe and Lupe, Esperanza finds that she now has to learn to change diapers and to wash clothes. In Mexico the servants washed her clothes. Even a simple task like sweeping the platform with a broom and dust pan is beyond Esperanza. Worse still, Marta draws people's attention to her ineptitude and calls her "'Cinderella!'" (117). Esperanza is humiliated when everyone laughs at her.

By the end of the chapter, Esperanza is determined to learn the menial skills that she has previously despised.

24. What reason does Esperanza give to Isabella for her belief that she will not be in the camp for long? What do we already know that makes us doubt that her confidence is realistic?

25. Mama explains that Hortensia and Alfonso have taken great trouble to help them in their time of need. Explain exactly what they have done to enable Esperanza and her mother to live and work at the camp.

26. Explain the contribution made by each of the following character's to the change of attitude to her situation that is evident in Esperanza by the end of the chapter: Mama, Isabella, Marta and Miguel.

21

Las Almendras (Almonds)

Alfonso and Miguel's secret is finally revealed. They have made a shrine to Our Lady of Guadalupe with a small garden of roses around it at the back of the cabin. The roses are the ones Papa planted, including the one for Miguel and for Esperanza. The shrine is a symbol of continuity, "Mama looked at Esperanza, 'Didn't I tell you that Papa's heart would find us wherever we go?'" (125). It seems that Miguel has in some ways replaced Papa in showing Esperanza that her life is connected to the life of the land because she is a part of nature.

Esperanza has always been bathed by Hortensia, but she now realizes that this is another thing she will have to do for herself. Her humiliation is, however, eased by Hortensia's kindness.

At the fiesta, Esperanza feels particularly alone since all of the groups seem to exclude her. Marta stands on the back of a truck and makes a speech urging everyone to join the strike that will take place in two weeks. Those who listen to her resist her message because they live in a camp that is better than average and they live there year-round, unlike the migrant pickers who have to move around California following the harvest. It is Isabella who, despite her youth, is able to explain this to Esperanza.

27. Marta and her mother are migrant workers who are currently picking cotton. In what ways is their life harder than that of the workers in the camp where Esperanza now lives?

28. How might a strike actually make the conditions of the laborers worse?

29. The chapter ends with a piece of ominous foreshadowing. Explain what Mama's final words might imply.

Esperanza Rising by Pam Muñoz Ryan

Las Ciruelas (Plums)

This novel is set during the years of the Great Dust Bowl in the early 1930s when the topsoil of the prairies, having been dried up by years of drought and impoverished by decades of planting the same crop, literally blew away. The areas most affected were the panhandles of Texas and Oklahoma and parts of New Mexico, Colorado, and Kansas. There have been several references in the novel to 'Okies' that is migrant workers from Oklahoma (and adjacent states) who have lost their farms and come to California to work as field laborers.

The dust storm in this chapter is not, however, part of the Dust Bowl. It is a feature of the San Joaquin Valley where intensive cultivation exposes the topsoil to wind erosion. One effect of the dust storm is to stop the strike that Marta has been supporting since all the work of picking cotton is halted because the crop is ruined.

30. For the first time, Esperanza is left alone to take care of the babies and to prepare dinner for everyone who is working. What mistakes does she make because of her lack of experience? How do the others react to discovering her mistakes when they get home?

31. Explain why the dust storm ends cotton picking for the season but does not affect the harvesting of grapes.

32. Explain how Esperanza's description of Melina (on page 144) shows her maturing understanding of life.

Las Papes (Potatoes)

With Mama not getting any better, and eventually having to go into hospital, Esperanza is forced to take responsibility. This is the lowest 'valley' in her fortunes, but it is also the turning point in her life because of the way that she reacts to it. For the first time she actually works in the sheds and does not complain about it. At the end of the chapter, she tells Mama, "'I will take care of everything, I will be *la patrona* for the family now'" (178). All of her life, she has relied on others to serve her, now she takes responsibility for her mother – their roles have been reversed. Her only failure in this chapter is that she cannot find a way to get a letter to Abuelita to tell her than Mama needs her to join them.

Working on the potatoes, the women discuss plans for a strike in the spring. The Mexican workers are split over the idea of striking: they all agree that they are not fairly rewarded for their work, but many have far too much to lose by striking – without their jobs they will not be able to buy food. This foreshadows problems that no one seems able to avoid.

33. Mama reminds Esperanza about Abuelita's blanket, and she resumes work on it. What is the significance of the pattern on the blanket? What other symbolic significance is there in Esperanza taking up the completion of the blanket that her grandmother started?
34. When Esperanza is telling Isabella about her childhood Christmases at El Rancho, she suddenly stops her story. At what point does she stop? What does her stopping her story at this point tell you about the way her character has developed?

Esperanza Rising by Pam Muñoz Ryan

Los Aguacates (Avocados)

Esperanza is forced to recognize that she is now a different person. No amount of avocados can give her back her soft hands; she now has "the hands of a poor *campesina*" (182). When she looks down at her ill-fitting, second-hand clothes and her tanned face, she understands why it does not occur to Americans that many Mexican immigrants have, as Miguel reminds her "'been trained in professions'" (187).

Miguel has also learned about racism in the U.S.A. He, more than Esperanza, has experienced insulting racism. Ironically, the one exception is Japanese immigrant store-keeper Mr. Yakota who treats Mexicans just as he treats everyone else. (Most readers will understand the irony of a Japanese American being more true to the ideals of the country than the native-born citizens, particularly since Japanese Americans would be interred during the Second World War because their loyalty was thought to be suspect.)

At Mr. Yakota's store, Esperanza buys a small piñata, thinking that it will hang above Mama's bed in the hospital and will cheer her up. However, when Esperanza encounters a hungry family of strikers, she gives the adults beans and gives the piñata to their children. This shows just how much Esperanza's character has developed, for only a few months earlier she would not even let a poor little girl hold her precious doll because she was afraid it would become dirty.

35. When Miguel is telling her that Americans think that all Mexicans are "uneducated, dirty, poor and unskilled" (187), Esperanza makes a joke at her own expense (the first time that she has ever done so). Explain the joke that she makes and what it suggests about the way Esperanza now sees herself.

36. How have the attitudes of Marta and Esperanza towards each other changed since they first met?

Los Espárragos (Asparagus)

This is a highly political chapter. In spring, the strikers renew their efforts and are met by the full resistance of the owners backed by the police and immigration officers. All of this is set against the background of rising numbers of migrant workers from the East flooding into California looking for work. These workers are so desperate for money that they are prepared to pick cotton at five or six cents per pound, which is below a livable wage. Because she is very intelligent, Esperanza understands what is happening. She realizes both how unfairly the poor are treated and how difficult it is for them to unite to take effective action to improve their wages and living conditions.

Esperanza has matured a lot in a very short time. Above all, she has learned how to feel empathy for people (the ability to put yourself in their place) who are different from her. It is especially significant that Esperanza gives the piñata to the children because she has previously been very selfish. At the beginning of the novel, she felt that poor people were almost a different species: dirty, rude and ignorant. She now understands that making a gift of the piñata is what Mama would want her to do.

When they go back to the farm where the strikers had been staying, Esperanza sees the piñata hanging from the tree in the midst of desolation. This shows how much the children must have had fun breaking open the piñata. However, the broken piñata also symbolizes the broken lives caused by the action taken against the strikers.

37. In their discussion of the strike, Esperanza says, "'That is the striker's point'" (204). What point is she drawing attention to? Why is it rather remarkable that she should have said this?

38. What methods do the police use in this chapter to ensure that the maximum numbers of Mexicans are deported?

39. Why does Esperanza save Marta? What does it show about Esperanza that she chooses to do this?

40. What might be symbolized by "the remains of the little donkey piñata that [Esperanza] had given to the children, its tissue streamers fluttering in the breeze … beaten with a stick, its insides torn out" (213).

Esperanza Rising by Pam Muñoz Ryan

Los Duraznos (Peaches)

At the beginning of this chapter, Esperanza comes close to despair as she watches those closest to her suffer from racist discrimination against which they are helpless: Isabel is cheated out of being Queen of the May, Miguel will never get the kind of skilled work that he deserves, and the Mexicans will only get to swim in the Okies' pool on the day before it gets cleaned. She is convinced that nothing will ever be right in the United States.

Esperanza gives Isabel her prized doll – the one that earlier she would not let a poor peasant girl touch because she was dirty. It is an action that shows her genuine care for Isabel. It also changes the relationship between the two. Up to this point, though younger by several years, Isabel has taken on the role of teacher to Esperanza, but now Esperanza reclaims the role of adult (or big sister) to Isabel acknowledging that she herself is "'much too old for dolls'" (228).

It is almost a year since Mama and Esperanza came from Mexico. Mama is finally released from hospital, but just when the novel seems in danger of falling into sentimentality, there is an abrupt plot-twist at the end of the chapter.

41. The chapter includes a number of examples of ways that the workers of Mexican heritage (whether or not they are American citizens) are victims of racial prejudice. Make a full list.

42. When Miguel and Esperanza argue about how he reacted to being replaced by an unqualified white man, their different viewpoints reflect the social classes they occupied in Mexico. Esperanza wants Miguel to fight for his rights, but Miguel believes that he must keep trying to prove his worth. She says he is "'still a peasant!'" and he says "'you still think you are a queen'" (224). Which of the two do you think is right?

43. Brainstorm possible explanations for the disappearance of Esperanza's savings.

Las Uvas (Grapes)

This chapter presents the resolution of the plot, which turns out to be a conventional 'happy ending'. Certainly, not everything is perfect: Abuelita has aged greatly in the time Mama and Esperanza have been in California; Mama, though much stronger, is unlikely to regain her former health; Miguel still has not got the sort of job for which he is qualified; the prospect of increasing numbers of migrant workers driving down wages still exists; the threat of strikes and of the owners' reaction is as real as ever; and so on.

A few days before her fourteenth birthday, Miguel takes Esperanza into the foothills. Together they lie down on the ground and each feels the beating of the earth. This is very different from Esperanza's failed attempt to hear the "heartbeat of the valley" when she first came to California (see pages 91-2). Then, she heard nothing. What she experiences now is the continuity of life which is guaranteed by the turning of the seasons of the year: everything that happens is part of everything else, and so nothing is ever lost. As a sign of this continuity, the novel ends with Esperanza teaching Isabel how to crochet, and giving Isabel the same advice Abuelita had once given to her when her stitches came out crooked: "Don't be afraid to start over" (15). This is the truth that Esperanza has learned about life.

44. At precisely what point did you guess what Miguel had done? Explain how you knew. Why do you think he did it?
45. In what ways is Esperanza's experience of flight different from the first time she had the feeling of "floating and drifting upward" (92)?
46. At the end of her 'flight', Esperanza has a vision of Miguel and herself. What is the most important detail of the vision? Explain.

Esperanza Rising by Pam Muñoz Ryan

Viewpoints:

Discuss each of the following judgments on the novel:
1. Publishers Weekly commented favorably on the "lyrical, fairy tale - like style." The review praised the way that "Ryan poetically conveys Esperanza's ties to the land by crafting her story to the rhythms of the seasons" and the fact that "Ryan fluidly juxtaposes world events ... with one family's will to survive." (Wikipedia article)
2. The Kirkus Review disliked the "epic tone, characters that develop little and predictably, and... [the] romantic patina [i.e. an impression or appearance of something]." (Wikipedia article)
3. "Pam Muñoz Ryan eloquently portrays the Mexican workers' plight in this abundant and passionate novel that gives voice to those who have historically been denied one." (Scholastic.com)
4. "[T]his literary masterpiece." (Schmoop.com)

Post-reading:

1. In the interview at the back of the book, Pam Muñoz Ryan says that one of the forms (genres) in which she writes is "magical realism." That term seems to be an oxymoron (i.e., a contradiction in terms). Find out what kind of writing is usually described as "magical realism." What incidents in this novel might be called "magical realism"?
2. Each chapter headings is the name of a fruit, vegetable, or other crop that has special meaning in that chapter. In the Q & A at the back of the book, the author explains how she came up with this idea. What was her intention? How effectively did it work for you?
3. *The Grapes of Wrath* by John Steinbeck tells the story of the Joad family, Okies thrown off their farm in the East who come to California to make a living picking fruit. It is rather a long book, and it written for adults, but you might consider reading it. Alternatively there is an old movie based on the novel that you might like to watch.
4. Draw a sketch giving your idea of the cabin in which Esperanza lives and the workers' camp.
5. Draw a map of Mexico and California and trace Esperanza's route .

Vocabulary

How do we learn new words?

In the first four years of your life you learned more words than you will learn in the rest of your life! You did this by listening to other people speak. Simply by hearing a word over and over again, you worked out what it meant. (That's why most babies say the words 'mommy' or 'daddy' first.)

As we get older, we still use this method to learn new words, but it doesn't work so well. That is because the words that we still do not know tend not to come up too often, so we don't get that repetition that helps us to work out what the words mean. (How many times are you likely to come across the word 'congregate' in the next month? It is in this novel, but you are unlikely to hear or read it again for a while!)

As a result, we have to make a deliberate effort to learn new words. Here is the best way:

- When you first see the word, try to relate it to other words that you already know. For example, 'mysticism' sounds like 'mystery' which means 'a puzzle, something unusual which does not have an obvious solution.'
- Look at the word in context. If you are able to relate it to a word that you know, does this meaning make any sense? Does the context add to your understanding of what the new word means?
- If you are unable to relate the word to one that you already knew, try reading the sentence with a blank where the new word goes. Ask yourself what word or phrase would you put into the blank to make sense in this context. Write your thoughts and guesses down.
- Check the dictionary definition of the word. How close were you?
- Remember that every word has a range of meanings. You need to know what the word means in the context in which it is used.

In selecting vocabulary from *Esperanza Rising*, I have chosen what I think are the most useful words.

Esperanza Rising by Pam Muñoz Ryan

VOCABULARY ACTIVITY ONE

1. draped, verb (1)   *Covered over by something (like a cloth or blanket).*

2. tendril, noun (1)   *Offshoot of a climbing plant that coils around a trellis.*

3. scythe, noun (4)   *Harvesting tool with a long curved blade on a long handle.*

4. fiesta, noun (6)   *Originally a religious festival, now any community celebration.*

5. anticipated, verb (8)   *Expected, predicted in advance, foreseen.*

6. premonition, noun (9) _____

7. serenaded, verb (9) _____

8. congregate, verb (9) _____

9. dwindled, verb (21) _____

10. transforming, verb (21) _____

11. wrenched, verb (23) _____

12. anguish, noun (23) _____

13. condolences, noun (26) _____

14. methodically, adj. (27) _____

15. encroaching, verb (29) _____

31

A Study Guide

VOCABULARY ACTIVITY TWO

1. composure, noun (29) *When a person is cool, calm and collected.*

2. indignation, noun (30) *Anger, resentment.*

3. devious, adj. (33) *Roundabout, underhand, behind someone's back.*

4. pungent, adj. (38) *Strong in smell or taste.*

5. smirk, noun (54) *A false smile; a smile that indicates self-satisfaction and pride.*

6. venom, noun (57) _____

7. debris, noun (110) _____

8. humiliation, noun (116) _____

9. extravagant, adj. (136) _____

10. immunized, verb (156) _____

11. indignation, noun (188) _____

12. discarded, verb (205) _____

13. infuriated, adj. (244) _____

14. unraveling, verb (253) _____

Esperanza Rising by Pam Muñoz Ryan

VOCABULARY TEST PART ONE

Below are some sentences. Select the word(s) from the vocabulary list that fits into each sentence. Some may be used more than once.

draped	tendril	scythe	fiesta
anticipated	premonition	serenaded	congregate
dwindled	wrenched	anguish	condolences
methodically	encroaching	transforming	

1. Having lost his library books, Paul decided to search his room _____ until he found them.

2. The student had not _____ that dissecting a frog would make her feel so nervous.

3. Before Titanic sailed on its first voyage, some passengers had a _____ of disaster.

4. The power of the tennis player's serve _____ the racquet out of my hand.

5. The defense lawyer set about _____ the way the jury saw his client.

6. At the end of the race, every exhausted rower in the boat was _____ over her oar.

7. Looking over the steep cliff, Roy was scared by a sudden _____ that he would fall.

8. Before every game, supporters would _____ in the parking lot.

9. The Senior Prom that year had to be cancelled because the number of students buying tickets _____ to one or two a day.

10. At the _____, Ellen's performance on guitar that got everyone dancing.

11. A sharp _____ will cut down long grass and weeds in no time.

12. The weeds from my neighbor's garden were gradually _____ into my own flower beds.

13. The _____ of her father's death was eased a little by the kind _____ that his daughter received.

33

14. It was a tradition that the married couple should be _____ by their friends.

15. A _____ from the rose had wound itself tightly around the other plants.

Esperanza Rising by Pam Muñoz Ryan

VOCABULARY TEST PART TWO

Below are some sentences. Select the word(s) from the vocabulary list that fits into each sentence. Some may be used more than once.

composure	indignation	devious	pungent
smirk	venom	debris	humiliation
extravagant	immunized	discarded	infuriated
unraveling			

1. The bite of the snake released poisonous _____ into his leg.

2. _____ from the crashed plane was visible over a wide area.

3. The umpire's incorrect call of strike _____ the batter.

4. He had a reputation for being _____ because he bought lots of luxuries that he did not need.

5. Fortunately it is now possible to be _____ against smallpox.

6. The ball of wool was _____ as the kitten pulled it across the room.

7. The _____ smell of orchids was almost overpowering.

8. The survivors in the lifeboat _____ everything that was not essential to their survival.

9. Although he felt _____ over his failure to win a medal, he vowed to try again next year.

10. There was a _____ on the student's face when she explained that the dog had eaten her homework.

11. He was _____ by the _____ way in which he was prevented from voting in the election.

12. The case for the defense began _____ as soon as the trial started.

13. Despite the great heat, the singer kept her _____ on stage.

A Study Guide

VOCABULARY TEST PART ONE - ANSWERS

draped	tendril	scythe	fiesta
anticipated	premonition	serenaded	congregate
dwindled	wrenched	anguish	condolences
methodically	encroaching	transforming	

1. Having lost his library books, Paul decided to search his room ***methodically*** until he found them.

2. The student had not ***anticipated*** that dissecting a frog would make her feel so nervous.

3. Before Titanic sailed on its first voyage, several passengers had a ***premonition*** of disaster.

4. The power of the tennis player's serve ***wrenched*** the racquet out of my hand.

5. The defense lawyer set about ***transforming*** the way the jury saw his client.

6. At the end of the race, each exhausted rower in the boat was ***draped*** over her oar.

7. Looking over the steep cliff, Roy was scared by a sudden ***premonition*** that he would fall.

8. Before every game, supporters would ***congregate*** in the parking lot.

9. The Senior Prom that year had to be cancelled because the number of students buying tickets ***dwindled*** to one or two a day.

10. At the ***fiesta***, Ellen's performance on guitar that got everyone dancing.

11. A sharp ***scythe*** will cut down long grass and weeds in no time.

12. The weeds from my neighbor's garden were gradually ***encroaching*** into my own flower beds.

13. The ***anguish*** of her father's death was eased a little by the kind ***condolences*** that she received.

14. It was a tradition that the married couple should be ***serenaded*** by their friends.

16. A ***tendril*** from the rose had wound itself tightly around the other plants.

VOCABULARY TEST PART TWO - ANSWERS

composure	indignation	devious	pungent
smirk	venom	debris	humiliation
extravagant	immunized	discarded	infuriated
unraveling			

1. The bite of the snake released poisonous ***venom*** into his leg.

2. ***Debris*** from the crashed plane was visible over a wide area.

3. The umpire's incorrect call of strike ***infuriated*** the batter.

4. He had a reputation for being ***extravagant*** because he bought lots of luxuries that he did not need.

5. Fortunately it is now possible to be ***immunized*** against smallpox.

6. The ball of wool was *unraveling* as the kitten pulled it across the room.

7. The *pungent* smell of orchids was almost overpowering.

8. The survivors in the lifeboat *discarded* everything that was not essential to their survival.

9. Although he felt *humiliation* over his failure to win a medal, he vowed to try again next year.

10. There was a *smirk* on the student's face when she explained that the dog had eaten her homework.

11. He was *infuriated* by the *devious* way in which he was prevented from voting in the election.

12. The case for the defense began *unraveling* as soon as the trial started.

13. Despite the great heat, the singer kept her *composure* on stage.

Appendix 1: Reading Group Use of the Study Guide Questions

Although there are both closed and open questions in the Study Guide, very few of them have simple, right or wrong answers. They are designed to encourage in-depth discussion, disagreement, and (eventually) consensus. Above all, they aim to encourage students to go to the text to support their conclusions and interpretations.

1. Set a reading assignment for the group and tell everyone to be aware that the questions will be the focus of whole group discussion at the next meeting.

2. Set a reading assignment for the group and allocate particular questions to sections of the group (e.g. if there are four questions, divide the group into four sections, etc.).

In the meeting, form discussion groups containing one person who has prepared each question and allow time for feedback within the groups.

Have feedback to the whole the on each question by picking a group at random to present their answers and to follow up with a group discussion.

3. Set a reading assignment for the group, but do not allocate questions.

In the meeting, divide readers into groups and allocate to each group one of the questions related to the reading assignment, the answer to which they will have to present formally to the meeting.

Allow time for discussion and preparation.

4. Set a reading assignment for the group, but do not allocate questions.

In the meeting, divide readers into groups and allocate to each group one of the questions related to the reading assignment.

Allow time for discussion and preparation.

Now reconfigure the groups so that each group contains at least one person who has prepared each question and allow time for feedback within the groups.

5. Before starting to read the text, allocate specific questions to individuals or pairs. (It is best not to allocate all questions to allow for other approaches and variety. One in three questions or one in four seems about right.) Tell readers that they will be leading the group discussion on their question. They will need to start with a brief presentation of the issues and then conduct a question and answer session. After this, they will be expected to present a brief review of the discussion.

6. Having finished the text, arrange the meeting into groups of 3, 4 or 5. Tell each group to select as many questions from the Study Guide as there are members of the group.

Each individual is responsible for drafting out an answer to one question, and each answer should be substantial.

Esperanza Rising by Pam Muñoz Ryan

Each group as a whole is then responsible for discussing, editing and suggesting improvements to each answer.

Appendix 2: Literary Terms relevant to this text

Allusion: a passing, brief or indirect reference to a well known person or place, or to something of historical, cultural, literary or political importance.

Ambiguous, ambiguity: when a statement is unclear in meaning – ambiguity may be deliberate or accidental.

Analogy: a comparison which treats two things as identical in one or more specified ways (e.g., "What's in a name? That which we call a rose / By any other word would smell as sweet" [Juliet in *Romeo and Juliet*].

Antagonist: a character or force opposing the protagonist.

Antithesis: the complete opposite of something (e.g., "Use every man after his *desert*, and who should 'scape *whipping*?" [Hamlet in *Hamlet*]).

Authorial comment: when the writer addresses the reader directly (not to be confused with the narrator doing so).

Climax: the conflict to which the action has been building since the start of the play or story.

Comic inversion: reversing the normally accepted order of language or of things for comic effect.

Connotation: the ideas, feelings and associations generated by a word or phrase or with an object or animal.

Dialogue: a conversation between two or more people in direct speech.

Diction: the writer's choice of particular words (the use of vocabulary) in order to create a particular effect.

First person: first person singular is "I" and plural is "we".

Foreshadowing: a statement or action which gives the reader a hint of what is likely to happen later in the narrative.

Genre: the type of literature into which a particular text falls (e.g. drama, poetry, novel).

Image, imagery: figurative language such as simile, metaphor, personification etc., or a description which conjures up a particularly vivid picture.

Imply, implication: when the text suggests to the reader a meaning which it does not actually state.

Infer, inference: the reader's act of going beyond what is stated in the text to draw conclusions.

Irony, ironic: a form of humor which undercuts the apparent meaning of a statement:

    Conscious irony: irony used deliberately by a writer or character;

Esperanza Rising by Pam Muñoz Ryan

Unconscious irony: a statement or action which has significance for the reader of which the character is unaware;

Dramatic irony: when an action has an important significance that is obvious to the reader but not to one or more of the characters;

Tragic irony: when a character says (or does) something which will have a serious, even fatal, consequence for him/ her. The audience is aware of the error, but the character is not;

Verbal irony: the conscious use of particular words which are appropriate to what is being said.

Image, imagery: figurative language such as simile, metaphor, personification etc., or a description which conjures up a particularly vivid picture.

Imply / implication: when the text suggests to the reader a meaning which it does not actually state.

Infer/ inference: the reader's act of going beyond what is stated in the text to draw conclusions.

Irony, ironic: a form of humor which undercuts the apparent meaning of a statement (e.g., Cassius is being ironic when he says of Julius Caesar, "'tis true this god did shake" [*Julius Caesar*]).

Juxtaposition: literally putting two things side by side for purposes of comparison and/ or contrast.

Literal: the surface level of meaning that a statement has.

Metaphor / metaphorical: the description of one thing by direct comparison with another (e.g. the coal-black night).

Extended metaphor: a comparison which is developed at length.

Motif: a frequently repeated idea, image or situation in a text.

Motivation: why a character acts as he/she does – in modern literature motivation is seen as psychological.

Narrator / Narrative voice: the voice that the reader hears in the text – not to be confused with the author.

Perspective: point of view from which a story, or an incident within a story, is told.

Personified / personification: a simile or metaphor in which an inanimate object or abstract idea is described by comparison with a human.

Plot: a chain of events linked by cause and effect.

Prologue: an introduction which gives a lead-in to the main story.

Protagonist: the character who initiates the action and is most likely to have the sympathy of the audience.

A Study Guide

Realism: a text that describes the action in a way that appears to reflect life.

Setting: the environment in which the narrative (or part of the narrative) takes place.

Simile: a description of one thing by explicit comparison with another (e.g., "My love is like a red, red rose" [Burns]).

> *Extended simile*: a comparison which is developed at length.

Style: the way in which a writer chooses to express him/ herself. Style is a vital aspect of meaning since how something is expressed can crucially affect what is being written or spoken.

Suspense: the building of tension in the reader.

Symbol, symbolic, symbolism, symbolize: a physical object which comes to represent an abstract idea (e.g. the sun may symbolize life).

Themes: important concepts, beliefs and ideas explored and presented in a text.

Third person: third person singular is "he/ she/ it" and plural is "they" – authors often write novels in the third person.

Tone: literally the sound of a text – how words sound (either in the mouth of an actor or the head of a reader) can crucially affect meaning.

Notes on Graphic Organizers

I would not want the reading of any work of literature to be reduced to filling in an endless stream of graphic organizers. On the other hand, these can be useful in helping readers to understand a text. Simply select the ones that you want to use.

I do *not* provide 'answers'. The students are *not* being asked to get to a pre-determined understanding of the text; they are being encouraged to develop their own understanding of it. It is much more important that they should compare their ideas in groups and compare their completed graphics with those of other students than that they should come up with some so-called 'right' answer.

Plot Graph

This is a simple representation of the rising and falling action. Students can place key incidents on the plot line.

Developing Perspectives

This allows readers to explore the starting point of the action and to understand how different characters relate to it.

Problem / Responses Table

Problems seldom have solutions either in real life or in fiction. In responding to one problem, other problems are created – that is what produces the series of cause-and-effect events that is the plot.

Esperanza Then and Now

The story of Esperanza is the story of how she is able to change when her life changes. This graphic allows students to build up a clear 'before and after' account of her character.

How Miguel shows that he cares for Esperanza

Because the story is told from Esperanza's point of view, it is easy to underestimate the role that Miguel plays in helping her.

A Study Guide

Plot graph for *Esperanza Rising*

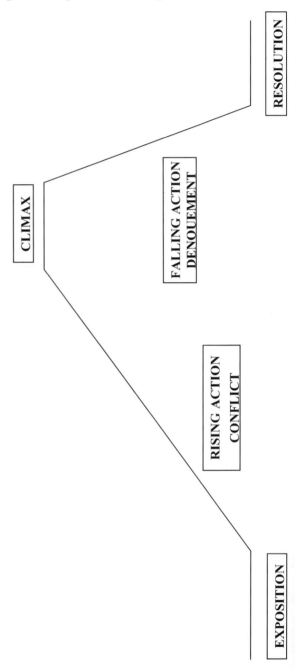

Esperanza Rising by Pam Muñoz Ryan

Developing perspectives on the situation which initiates the action in the novel

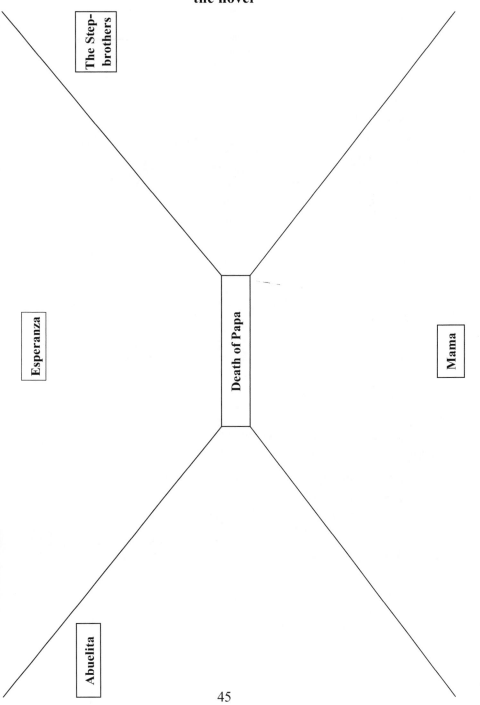

The Step-brothers

Esperanza

Death of Papa

Mama

Abuelita

A Study Guide

Plot development

Complete the response for each problem to show the development of the plot.

Problem	Responses
Las Uvas (Grapes) Papa is late returning from his work on the farm	
Las Papayas (Papayas) Papa's will leaves the ranch land to Tío Louis	
Los Higos (Figs) The house is burned down and the brothers threaten more burnings	
Las Guayabas (Guavas) Mama decides to take the family to California	
Los Melones (Cantaloupes) Esperanza faces life in a place and with people she does not know	
Las Cebollas (Onions) Esperanza has to do tasks that she has never done before	
Las Almendras (Almonds) Marta makes a speech in the camp encouraging the workers to go on strike	

Las Ciruelas (Plums) Mama gets sick with Valley Fever	
Las Papes (Potatoes) Mama has to go to hospital and will be there for a long time	
Los Aguacates (Avocados) More and more poor workers come into the valley who will work for less money than the Mexicans	
Los Espárragos (Asparagus) The strike starts and the police take strong (sometimes illegal) action against the strikers	
Los Duraznos (Peaches) Isabel desperately wants to be chosen by her teacher as Queen of the May	
Las Uvas (Grapes) Esperanza finds that the money she has saved to bring Abuelitato California has been stolen	

A Study Guide

Esperanza Then and Now

	In the first four chapters	By the final chapter
1. Social position		
2. Relationship with her family members		
3. Relationship with servants		
4. Attitude to poor people		
5. Attitude to work		
6. Relationship with Miguel		
7. Relationship with the earth		
8. Understanding of what is important in life		
9.		
10.		

Esperanza Rising by Pam Muñoz Ryan

How Miguel shows that he cares for Esperanza

Miguel is in love with Esperanza, and throughout the story he shows how much he cares for her. On the timeline make a list of *all* the things he does to support her both emotionally and practically. (To start, here is an *incomplete* list in no particular order: takes roses from her father's garden and creates a shrine behind her cabin; finds her a job in the packing shed when she needs to earn money; takes the risk of returning to Mexico to bring Abuelita to California; etc.)

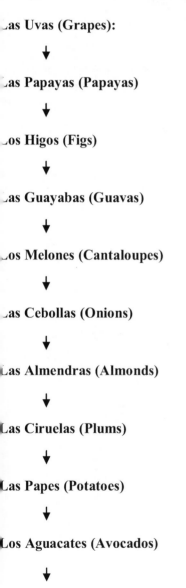

Las Uvas (Grapes):

↓

Las Papayas (Papayas)

↓

Los Higos (Figs)

↓

Las Guayabas (Guavas)

↓

Los Melones (Cantaloupes)

↓

Las Cebollas (Onions)

↓

Las Almendras (Almonds)

↓

Las Ciruelas (Plums)

↓

Las Papes (Potatoes)

↓

Los Aguacates (Avocados)

↓

Los Espárragos (Asparagus)

↓

Los Duraznos (Peaches)

↓

Las Uvas (Grapes)

↓

To the Reader

Ray strives to make his products the best that they can be. If you have any comments or questions about this book *please* contact the author through his email: **moore.ray1@yahoo.com**

Visit his website at **http://www.raymooreauthor.com**

Also by Ray Moore: Most books are available from amazon.com as paperbacks and at most online eBook retailers.

Fiction:

The Lyle Thorne Mysteries: each book features five tales from the Golden Age of Detection:

Investigations of The Reverend Lyle Thorne
Further Investigations of The Reverend Lyle Thorne
Early Investigations of Lyle Thorne
Sanditon Investigations of The Reverend Lyle Thorne
Final Investigations of The Reverend Lyle Thorne

Non-fiction:

The ***Critical Introduction series*** is written for high school teachers and students and for college undergraduates. Each volume gives an in-depth analysis of a key text:

"The Stranger" by Albert Camus: A Critical Introduction (Revised Second Edition)
"The General Prologue" by Geoffrey Chaucer: A Critical Introduction
"Pride and Prejudice" by Jane Austen: A Critical Introduction
"The Great Gatsby" by F. Scott Fitzgerald: A Critical Introduction

The Text and Critical Introduction series differs from the Critical introduction series as these books contain the original text and in the case of the medieval texts an interlinear translation to aid the understanding of the text. The commentary allows the reader to develop a deeper understanding of the text and themes within the text.

"Sir Gawain and the Green Knight": Text and Critical Introduction
"The General Prologue" by Geoffrey Chaucer: Text and Critical Introduction
"The Wife of Bath's Prologue and Tale" by Geoffrey Chaucer: Text and Critical Introduction
"Heart of Darkness" by Joseph Conrad: Text and Critical Introduction
"The Sign of Four" by Sir Arthur Conan Doyle Text and Critical Introduction
"A Room with a View" By E.M. Forster: Text and Critical Introduction
"Oedipus Rex" by Sophocles: Text and Critical Introduction
"Henry V" by William Shakespeare: Text and Critical Introduction

51

A Study Guide

Study guides available in print- listed alphabetically by author
* denotes also available as an eBook
"ME and EARL and the Dying GIRL" by Jesse Andrews: A Study Guide
"Wuthering Heights" by Emily Brontë: A Study Guide *
"Jane Eyre" by Charlotte Brontë: A Study Guide *
"The Myth of Sisyphus" and "The Stranger" by Albert Camus: Two Study Guides *
"The Meursault Investigation" by Kamel Daoud: A Study Guide
"Great Expectations" by Charles Dickens: A Study Guide *
"The Sign of Four" by Sir Arthur Conan Doyle: A Study Guide *
"The Wasteland, Prufrock and Poems" by T.S. Eliot: A Study Guide
"A Room with a View" by E. M. Forster: A Study Guide
"Looking for Alaska" by John Green: A Study Guide
"Paper Towns" by John Green: A Study Guide
"Catch-22" by Joseph Heller: A Study Guide *
"Unbroken" by Laura Hillenbrand: A Study Guide
"The Kite Runner" by Khaled Hosseini: A Study Guide
"A Thousand Splendid Suns" by Khaled Hosseini: A Study Guide
"Go Set a Watchman" by Harper Lee: A Study Guide
"On the Road" by Jack Keruoac: A Study Guide
"Life of Pi" by Yann Martel: A Study Guide *
"The Secret Life of Bees" by Sue Monk Kidd: A Study Guide
"Selected Poems" by Sylvia Plath: A Study Guide *
"An Inspector Calls" by J.B. Priestley: A Study Guide
"The Catcher in the Rye" by J.D. Salinger: A Study Guide
"Henry V" by William Shakespeare: A Study Guide
"Macbeth" by William Shakespeare: A Study Guide *
"Othello" by William Shakespeare: A Study Guide *
"Antigone" by Sophocles: A Study Guide *
"Oedipus Rex" by Sophocles: A Study Guide
"Cannery Row" by John Steinbeck: A Study Guide
"East of Eden" by John Steinbeck: A Study Guide
"Of Mice and Men" by John Steinbeck: A Study Guide *
"The Bridge of San Luis Rey" by Thornton Wilder: A Study Guide *
Study Guides available as e-books:
"Heart of Darkness" by Joseph Conrad: A Study Guide
"The Mill on the Floss" by George Eliot: A Study Guide
"Lord of the Flies" by William Golding: A Study Guide
"Nineteen Eighty-Four" by George Orwell: A Study Guide
"Henry IV Part 2" by William Shakespeare: A Study Guide
"Julius Caesar" by William Shakespeare: A Study Guide
"The Pearl" by John Steinbeck: A Study Guide

Esperanza Rising by Pam Muñoz Ryan

"Slaughterhouse-Five" by Kurt Vonnegut: A Study Guide

Teacher resources: Ray also publishes many more study guides and other resources for classroom use on the 'Teachers Pay Teachers' website: **http://www.teacherspayteachers.com/Store/Raymond-Moore**

Made in the USA
San Bernardino, CA
11 May 2020

71173800R00033